MARTHA STUART'S *BETTER THAN YOU AT*
ENTERTAINING

by Tom Connor & Jim Downey

Photographs by J. Barry O'Rourke

HarperPerennial
A Division of HarperCollinsPublishers

MARTHA STUART'S *BETTER THAN YOU AT* ENTERTAINING
By Tom Connor & Jim Downey

A parody of Martha Stewart's "Entertaining" and "Special Occasions" books.

Tom Connor & Jim Downey are also the authors of *Is Martha Stuart Living?* (HarperPerennial, 1995).
They live with their wives and children in Connecticut.

HarperCollins books may be purchased for educational, business or sales promotional use. For information, please write:
Special Markets Department, HarperCollins Publishers, Inc., 10 East 53rd Street, New York, NY 10022.

FIRST EDITION

Designed by Tom Connor, Jim Downey & Laura Campbell

All photographs copyright © 1996 by J. Barry O'Rourke except page 22: The National Audubon Society Collection

ISBN 0-06-095171-0

96 97 98 99 00 ❖/RRD 10 9 8 7 6 5 4 3 2

ACKNOWLEDGMENTS

Doing all that I do, as well as I do it, occasionally requires some assistance from others. In recognition, therefore, of limited contributions but in lieu of compensation in any other form and disavowing their rights to or royalties from any thought, concept, idea, product or service associated with me, my company or its subsidiaries in the United States, Eastern Europe, the World Wide Web or on other planets, now and in perpetuity, I hereby acknowledge:

Darryl Hooey for his help in converting the Appaloosa herd to glue for my glueguns; Suzy Pemberton, Missy Hofner, Sally Grimm, Bitsy Farnswirth, Felicia Lambastico and Lance Porcelli for standing in as look-alikes for me at book signings and Kmart appearances; my bodyguards Paulie, Joey "Six Fingers," Shecky, Vinnie "The Trowel," and Frankie and Annette; my gardener, Karl Simsbury, whom I hear is recovering nicely from his accident with the electrified fence and subsequent nervous breakdown; William "Whacky" Thruxtonheimer, whose artistry with a weed whacker is unparalleled in the industry; Betsey, my personal assistant, for going to the bathroom for me; Paulo Ramirez, matador and teacher, for showing me the proper way to run with the bulls in Pamplona, among other things; Nancy MacPherson-Schwartz, for tirelessly trying to match the stain on the outbuildings with the color of the chicken manure; His Holiness Pope John Paul George for demonstrating to the world that Polishness is next to Godliness; my kitchen staff, gardening staff, magazine staff, chauffeurs, personal trainers; my butcher, my baker, my candlestick maker; the Olatunji Gold Mine in South Africa for supplying me with gold leaf; and, oh yes, my mother, without whom the world would not have me.

CONTENTS

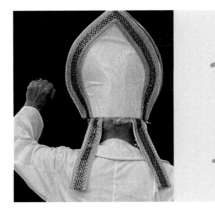

5 mother's day
homestyle dinner & payback

Tuna Casserole with Potato Chip Topping

Green Bean & Mushroom Soup Casserole
with Onion Rings

Salisbury Steak Croquettes

Sweet Potatoes with Marshmallows

Jell-O Aquarium Mold

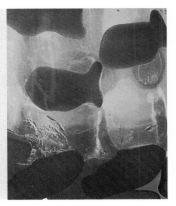

6 4th of july
beach cookout

Lobster au Villain

Freshly Caught Record Striped Bass
with Cucumber Scales

Ragout of Seaweed

Truman Compote

7 all souls' day
a death at dinner & impromptu wake

Mortadeli on Caskets of Toast

Blackened Dead Sea Scallops

Cold Funeral Meats

Stiffened Lady Fingers in Ice Cream

MARTHA'S EMBALMSAMIC VINAIGRETTE

8 christmas
holiday buffet & ornament-making party

Traditional Polish Christmas Wreath
Hors d'Oeuvres

Branded & Roasted
Limited-Range Wild Turkey

Snow Peas, Winter Squash,
Cold Brussels Sprouts

Martha's Eggnog

Baba au Rhum Das

INTRODUCTION

Over the years I've come to be known as many things: the Ice Queen, Our Lady of Perpetual Gilt, the Dominatrix of Domesticity, Elle Duce, Mothra Stuart, Martha de Sade, Shiitake Mushrooms-for-Brains. But how I perceived myself as a young girl, and how I hope to be remembered, is as a teacher.

A recent study of high school home economics courses in the United States found an alarming 23 percent drop in performance over the past five years. As a result, American teenage girls now rank well below Kurdistanian shepherds' daughters in baking skills. American mothers score even lower on basic housekeeping tests: Spot inspections by my staff of suburban homes around the nation revealed store-bought poultry and eggs, unstenciled walls and floors, ungilded things, and under some beds dustballs the size of Volvos.

Simply put, people's lives would be better if they would only do what I instruct them to do.

Each of the occasions featured in the pages of this book contains lesson plans, if you will, for perfect living. I strongly urge you to study and commit them to memory. There are those of you, I know, who make fun of me for my standards and accomplishments. But when I'm named Teacher of the Year and declare a state of Martha Law, you'll be spending time with me in detention.

easter

papal visit
& luncheon

communion wafers with caviar

homemade wine from water

puttanesca

loaves & fishes

lamb de dieu

1

THE POPE NEVER FAILS to pay his respects
when touring North America. His Holiness
knows he will always find a warm
welcome, a chaste and perfect home
and some of his favorite Polish foods.

{Entertaining Tips

Receiving a Pontiff in your home is really no different than entertaining royalty or anyone else in high office. But most of what is involved is basic good entertaining sense of the kind I've always demonstrated.

1. BE YOURSELF. *When Queen Elizabeth stopped by last spring, I made her some tea, then went right back to restoring a nineteenth-century bidet for use as a soup tureen. And when one of the Queen's corgies ran through my iris garden, nearly ruining the day's video shoot, I did what I would have done had it been the next-door neighbor's dog (see recipe for Roast Corgi).*

2. MAKE GUESTS FEEL AT HOME. *Few things permit important guests to relax more than knowing that their hostess understands what it's like to be them. That's why I lord over my staff, abuse tradespeople and in general behave like Leona Helmsley on angel dust.*

3. OBSERVE YOUR GUESTS CLOSELY. *Many people believe that royalty is above filching a piece of silver or china, but this simply isn't true. Even if I, if left alone in your living room, spot a saltbox or figurine I need, you'll never see that thing again—it's gone, it's mine. However, this doesn't absolve others from inappropriate behavior. Once, late at night, I caught Princess Di stealing a wedge of pie the size of Wales out of the refrigerator and had to whack her a good half dozen times on the hand with a spatula before she gave it up.*

LOAVES AND FISHES

The Pope's visit was a perfect excuse to try out a new fishing rod I had just designed. In 20 minutes my creel was full of the ocean's bounty.

TO SERVE MULTITUDES

    homebaked loaves

    several species of freshly caught fish

1. Blanch the fish for about 3 minutes and 10 seconds in any French copper pot over a gas range. This will cook them just past the sushi stage, while killing any botulism present.

2. Let the fishes cool to room temperature, occasionally rubbing them with a chamois cloth soaked in extra virgin olive oil to preserve their shine.

3. Serve unseasoned between a variety of homemade peasant breads.

LAMB DE DIEU

This is a variation on a biblical dish that I thought the Pontiff would appreciate.

TO SERVE TWO

    1 lamb

    40 heads of garlic

    1/2 lb. Dead Sea salt

    bitter herbs

1. Cull the tenderest-looking lamb from your flock. This takes concentration. The lamb you want will avoid any eye contact with you and attempt to hide behind its mother. Be patient: The smart ones taste best.

2. Kill, skin (save pelt for slipper stocking stuffers at Christmas), gut and remove one leg. (Give the other one to the guard dogs if they've been doing a good job.)

3. Make 365 (one for each day) 1/2-inch-deep slits in the leg and insert one clove of garlic into each slit.

4. Rub salt into the wounds, followed by bitter herbs.

5. Cook outside on a spit over a fire of Jerusalem cyprus wood for the period from matins to vespers.

A multitude of loaves and fishes proves ideal for serving the kind of crowds that can be expected whenever the Pontiff visits. It's also a meal which, by charging $20 per head (plus fees for admission, rides, religious items and souvenirs), can turn quite a tidy little profit.

Wafer & Caviar}
Assembly

Pipe a charming religious icon onto the side of the wafer marked with a cross, taking care not to crack the delicate surface. I prefer 1/16th of an inch, but feel free to use thicker lines to taste.

After choosing an appropriate pattern—a cross, Easter egg, symbolic fish, God, me—etch the skin of the cream cheese with a knifepoint or nail file. I've also found that an old diamond-tipped Victrola needle, taped or glued to an index fingertip, makes a wonderful scribing instrument.

With a pair of tweezers (and a magnifying glass if necessary), lay eggs a centimeter apart over the pattern until the design is complete.

What began as friendly competition} *soon turned to deep frustration (above) and a nice Merlot (below).*

*Hearing sins and personal failures
is just one of my many duties at Easter time.*

{Turning Water into Wine

When the Pope and I ran out of things to talk about after a minute or two, I thought I'd ask him to demonstrate his method for making wine from water the old-fashioned way. I furnished him with a sufficient amount of my best tap water, then stood back and waited for what I hoped would turn out to be an '89 Petrus or, at worst, a Nouveau Beaujolais.

John Paul George must have been having a bad day because, try as he might, after about twenty minutes I was still looking at two glasses of water and a sorry excuse for a Pontiff.

Here's my method:
Start with good glassware and fresh, home-made water. Sit down, compose yourself, and remember that this is not a big deal. Concentrate on the water while saying to yourself, "This is only water, I made it, I can make it into something else." Then—and this may be the difficult part for the average person—I place my hands over the water and direct most but certainly not all of my powers through my fingertips. Through sheer force of will, I now insist that the water become wine —in this case, a lovely Merlot. I am always pleasantly pleased with the results.

PUTTANESCA

While not traditional Polish fare, this classic spicy pasta has been a favorite of popes and Vatican officials for centuries. Its busty aroma and saucy, pungent flavor deliver a real bang. The secret is in the olive oil, which must be pressed from olives grown in the alleys of Naples. The exact literal translation of "Puttanesca" escapes me, but some young Italian friends tell me the dish derives its name from a group of working women who would make this dish to lure prospective husbands.

TO SERVE TWO

    1/2 cup extra nonvirgin olive oil

    2 dozen anchovy fillets

    enough garlic to ward off the Devil

    plum tomatoes (East Hampton garden)

    1 small berry basket of capers from caperbush
      (Westport garden)

    black olives, coarsely chopped (Rome estate grove)

    coarsely ground pepper from pepperbush
      (Fairfield herb garden)

    capellitto #27

1. Harvest ingredients morning of dinner.

2. Mash garlic, anchovies and oil in a pestle for several hours or until your forearm is the size of mine.

3. Dump paste in a saucepan and add capers, tomatoes and olives. Stir and heat over medium fire, then simmer uncovered over low heat on pasta stove for 11 hours. Pepper to taste.

4. Place eight ounces of capellitto in pot of boiling water for nine minutes.

5. Spoon sauce over mound of pasta in a suggestive way.

6. Serve with wine, bread and cheese accompanied by the Dean Martin recording of "That's Amore."

labor day

a gardening party

hand-picked field salad

smoked woodchuck

Martha's bug juice

compost cake

GARDEN SETTING: A hand cultivator, trowel and weed digger set the tone for this special end-of-summer occasion in the garden, where much work is to be done before lunch.

Each summer I invite the chapter presidents of The Martha Stuart Fan Clubs from around the country (and soon to be the world) to one of my homes for a luncheon and day of quality time with me. It's my way of acknowledging these special women for their Doberman-like allegiance to all that I represent, and for buying $15,000 or more of my products at Kmart.

Left, club founder and National President Bernice McCracken shown with her proud husband, Delbert, who followed her from their home in Lima Bean, Indiana.

Unidentified berries and fresh lawn capers spice up an all-natural salad found around my Connecticut property.

{Collecting Fans

Fan clubs were once considered tasteless as well as senseless, the stuff of teen idols and Hollywood types. That was before a small gathering of middle-class suburban housewives with time on their hands and zero ideas in their heads formed the first chapter of The Martha Stuart Fan Club.

Now, fan clubs make perfect sense.

Fans don't judge you for who you are, only for whom you appear to be. Loyal fans don't abandon you for someone younger, leaving you feeling like an empty tuna mousse mold. They tend to purchase everything you endorse, regardless of how expensive or impractical it may be. Last but not least, devoted fans make excellent workers. The trick is to make fans feel they're an important part of your life without allowing them ever to touch you or you them. A heavy pair of gardening gloves can prevent most contact.

While fans don't grow on fruit trees (well, some do), they can be found all over America: in malls and Kmarts, in tract houses and trailer parks, in raised ranches, Tudor condos and Winnebagos. Wherever there are women dissatisfied with how they live, with who they are and who they are not, that is where you'll find potential fans of mine. By simply belonging to my fan club, they need no longer worry about who they're not, because I'm who they're not.

Here are a few basic tips for collecting and maintaining fans:

1. *Take basic household tasks women have been doing thanklessly for centuries, make them even more time- and labor-intensive, then romanticize them.*

2. *Marry someone with a last name less ethnic than yours, and order the best stationery you can afford.*

3. *Hire an advertising agency, public relations firm, image consultant, damage control manager, media spin specialist, lobbyists, dates, bodyguards, and celebrity lookalikes.*

4. *Practice giving the impression you have a sense of humor about yourself and life, even though you know there's absolutely nothing funny about them.*

5. *Be human, but not too human. Always leave open the possibility of enrolling fans in the religion you've been thinking about establishing.*

MARTHA'S BUG JUICE

Remember summer camp and the big, cool, stainless steel pots of sweet, red liquid we called bug juice? In the early 1950s, in what was one of my first retailing successes, I "cleaned up" selling batches of my own brand of this classic childhood drink to fellow campers.

Early experimentation catching and squashing insects led me to discover the special properties of powdered ladybug shells. When mixed with warm pond water, sugar borrowed from the camp kitchen and various commercial dyes, I found they made a delicious, refreshing, mildly addictive drink. And, by charging first five cents a cup, then steadily upping the price with rising demand, by the end of the summer every child at camp was gladly forking over her birthday checks and care packages from home in exchange for a sip.

Here is how I make it:

TO SERVE AN ENTIRE CAMP OR FAN CLUB

    10 mason jars of ladybug shells
    20 gallons stagnant pond, lake or medium-brown
        river water
    10 pounds white sugar
    red dyes #17, 49, 101 and 230
    2 jars lightning bugs (optional)
    1 gallon Polish vodka

1. Capture ladybugs and pull off their shells. Store in mason jars.
2. Empty jars into industrial kitchen vats.
3. Add pond water, sugar and dyes.
4. Stir with canoe paddle.
5. Float vodka on surface until it resembles a toxic spill.
6. Ladle mixture out into six-ounce Dixie cups.
7. Have addicts begin preparing next batch.

HAND-PICKED FIELD SALAD

Salads fresh from the garden and lawn are simple to make and can be thrown together at the very last minute—perfect fare for hungry guests, gardeners or guest gardeners. Be sure to stop spraying with fungicides and pesticides at least an hour before lunch is to be served.

TO SERVE EIGHT

    1 bucket assorted marigold deadheads
    2 piles of mulch
    roots of 12 dozen dandelions
    1 cup peat moss
    1 bucket milkweed pods
    3 cups wild birdseed
    wren or catbird nest from boxwood hedge
    lawn capers (rabbit or deer) to taste

1. Hose down leafy weeds and hang on line to dry.
2. Empty weed buckets and mower bag into a livestock trough, then wash thoroughly using a garden hose.
3. Dump in a gallon of LawnBoy salad dressing.
4. Add milkweed pods, peat moss and lawn capers.
5. On a concrete slab or section of slate garden path, bake pods and birdseed in sun for an hour and a half or until crunchy. Cool on leaf tarp or swimming pool cover, then toss on top of greens.
6. Mix ingredients with pitchfork. Serve on clay flowerpot saucers.

Smoked Woodchuck

For many years I laid complex plans and set devious traps for eliminating that pesky intruder, the common groundhog or woodchuck, from my gardens. Most satisfying was the miniature guillotine I once placed at the main entrance to a critter's underground lair, which I then rigged with an enticing radicchio and endive salad attached to a trip wire.

The inevitable problem, of course, was what to do with the headless carcass. An equal problem over the years has been what to do with the mindless carcasses of fan club members who pop up on my property like gophers in heat. Last spring, however, I finally came up with the perfect solution to both challenging situations: smoke the chuck in its hole, then serve it to the clunkheads.

A timeless gardeners' staple, this course must be prepared in the following manner:

TO SERVE FOUR TO EIGHT
> 1 very large or half a dozen small woodchucks, groundhogs, hedgehogs or otherwise available vermin
> 50-gallon drum of Persian Gulf Lighter Fluid or liquid napalm
> 10 bags Martha's Own Charcoal

1. First, block off the rodent's auxiliary entrance and emergency exit by backing your cement mixer up to the holes and dumping down a fresh load of concrete.
2. Now pour five to ten large bags of my applewood charcoal brickets into the main entrance and pump in the lighter fluid.
3. Seal the entrance with a tarpaulin and cinder blocks, leaving only enough room to toss in a lit match or fire a blast from your flamethrower.
4. Leave the property for two to three days.
5. On the third day return to the garden, peel back the tarp and probe into the hole with a sharpened shark gaff to retrieve the smoking carcass. Transport to the picnic table in a wheelbarrow.
6. Remove remaining tufts of hair with a weed whacker.
7. Slice breast meat with a scythe or pull off hind and forelegs to eat off the bone.

The common North American woodchuck is found in most gardens, where it selects the tenderest shoots and fruits. But when smoked and sliced (as with this former resident of my Westport garden), woodchuck strongly resembles young goat meat. Which is just what my fan club chapter presidents believed they were having for lunch.

COMPOST CAKE

This entertaining little dessert demands months of preparation but never fails to intrigue guest-gardeners.

TO SERVE EIGHT

    8 pounds bitter dark chocolate, coarsely
        grated to simulate compost soil

    4 sticks shortbread for corner posts

    2 pounds marzipan for rotting vegetables

    1 pound nougat for chain-link fence

    6 tubes of white and green icing for
        climbing ivy, carrot tops, etc.

    1/2 pound hand-milled flour

    6 Parisian squab eggs

    2 tubs fresh Mexican burro butter

    2 cups Himalayan yak milk

1. Using the white from a freshly laid mallard egg, glue the 1"x1" corner shortbread posts to a foot-long section of rolled, flattened and hardened Bonomo's Turkish Taffy.

2. Construct compost bin by weaving strands of spun nougat into four-inch-high chain-link fencing on three sides. "Grow" climbing ivy icing up fence.

3. Begin depositing successive layers of grated chocolate six to eight months prior to baking.

4. Periodically add to the pile any partially eaten cake and cookies taken from weddings and restaurants, candy wrappers, crumbs found in pockets and purses, etc.

5. Two weeks before the gardening party, start fashioning composted marzipan items such as banana peels, sprouting potatoes, funguses and mushrooms.

6. Pour flour, squab eggs, burro butter and yak milk onto pile and let saturate in the backyard for one week.

7. Heat from the composting process should bake most of the cake, but to ensure a dry middle hold an acetylene torch to the bottom for about 20 seconds.

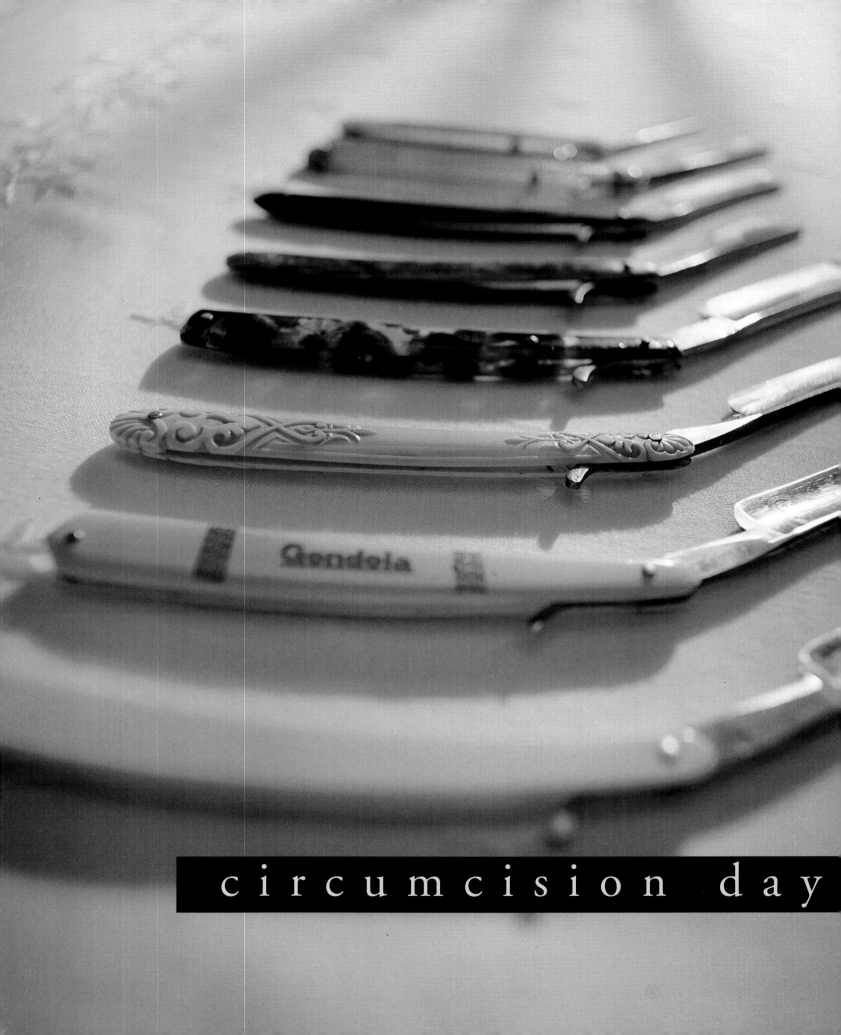

circumcision day

home ceremony

& hors d'oeuvres

cocktail wieners with
Swedish meatballs

calamari tips in red sauce

alcoholic beverages

A PERSONAL COLLECTION of antique
straight-edge razors, assertively laid out
on the dining room table, lends authority
to a variety of occasions and comes in
handy for circumcisions, vasectomies and
other simple home procedures.

{ Tips

I frequently get asked by new parents, wary of the general incompetence of doctors, to help get their newborn sons off to a perfect start in life by performing this most basic of male rituals. Having witnessed some shoddy work in this area, I first took up circumcision as a hobby but quickly found my services in great demand by parents across the country. And with good reason. Being able to say that your son was circumsised by Martha Stuart has a certain cachet.

Instead of the usual somber and somewhat unpleasant occasion usually associated with this procedure, I see it as an opportunity for a celebration. The home setting, the array of excitingly sharp razors, the special hors d'oeuvres and bright red sauces, add up to an unforgettable moment for all those involved, especially the infant. And while this isn't a skill that's usable on an everyday basis, it's well worth learning. I never leave the house without a razor or two.

Here are some tips, so to speak, on cleanliness and parental management:

1. *The day before the circumcision, bring in an environmental clean-up crew to thoroughly disinfect the kitchen area. This accomplishes two things: It ensures a germ-free area for the safety of the infant, and it tends to nip any potential lawsuits in the bud.*

2. *The father will invariably insist that he be on-site for the procedure. In my experience, however, all men are wimps, and as soon as he sees the razor come out he'll hit the floor like a sack of warm fertilizer. If possible, then, keep the father away from the action. If he insists on staying, pre-anesthetize him with a liter of good homemade whiskey.*

3. *The mother frequently asks if I can work in some design element, such as a scalloped or filigreed edge. But it is my feeling that this is one of those occasions where less is more, and that it's better to remain traditional. If she continues to give you a hard time, simply hand her the razor. You won't hear another peep.*

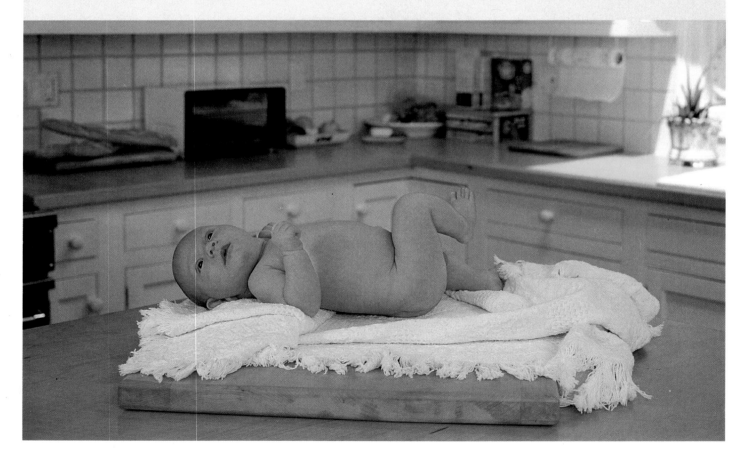

COCKTAIL WIENERS WITH SWEDISH MEATBALLS

Cocktail wieners provide a wonderful opportunity to finally rid the refrigerator of everything you can no longer identify.

On similar occasions in the past, I've used full-size, ballpark-style frankfurters, even a bratwurst with very large meatballs. But in general, it's best to keep the scale small so as not to offend.

TO SERVE SIX TO EIGHT

    1 1/2 pounds mixed meat

    1 pound salt

    1 yard of intestines

1. Take 1 1/2 pounds of any meat product from any animal, along with fat trimmings and skimmed fat, cartilage, gelatin, gristle and tendons and puree in a six-horsepower blender until it is about the consistency of lava.

2. Add the salt.

3. Pipe the mixture into a three-foot-long, 1/2-inch-diameter length of a newborn calf's intestine using a pastry bag and large tip.

4. Tie off two-inch sections and boil the entire piece until it turns grey or reaches a temperature of 212 degrees to kill every living thing in there. Cool to room temperature and cut into individual wieners.

FOR MEATBALLS, ADD ONE POUND OF BURGER MEAT

1. Roll into balls about the size of a small Fabergé egg.

2. Sear in a Belgian cast-iron skillet until the outside of the meatballs is the color of Aristotle's hat in the Rembrandt painting *Aristotle Contemplating the Bust of Homer.*

3. Arrange wieners and meatballs as units in a natural manner.

{ Keeping Razors Circumcision-Sharp

There is a right and a wrong way to sharpen everything from a pitchfork to a pencil. With razors (and to avoid excessive, loud, distracting or generally distasteful crying on the part of the infant), it is imperative that they be exquisitely sharp. I know my razor is sharp if I can split a Russian sable hair into four pieces lengthwise. The sharpening method I employ is the same one used by k. d. lang, who enjoys a close shave.

First, wait until one of your old stud bulls dies, then tan his hide using the South Dakota Blackfoot Indian tanning process (see my book Martha Stuart's Neutering & Tanning Occasions). *Once the hide has been tanned, cut an eight-inch-by-four-foot-long strip and let it sit on your roof for one year. Use the rest of the hide for home-made bull jerky. Now, using thongs made by braiding rawhide and Gore-Tex, fashion loops at either end, place a foot through one and hold the other to make a superb strop. The key here is to strop only in one direction, with 3000 strokes per side. This is a somewhat repetitive task, so I try to do it during my hour or two of sleep a night.*

Since steel takes a better edge when cold, I keep my razors in the vegetable crisper section of my refrigerator until ready to sharpen. You should do the same.

$\mathcal{C}$ALAMARI TIPS IN RED SAUCE

The delicate tips and ringlets of blanched squid make for tasty Circumcision Day nibblets.

TO SERVE PARENTS & GUESTS

    6 North Atlantic baby squid

    3 dozen Trieste-grown, organic Italian tomatoes

    salt, pepper, oregano, palmetto leaves to taste

    cheap red wine

1. Wash and eviscerate squid in a surgical stainless steel sink. Throw the entrails onto compost heap.
2. Boil for 7 minutes 11 seconds.
3. Quickly remove from pot and submerge in cold ocean water (Bay of Fundy water is excellent for this).
4. Slice off tips and make ringlets with a surgical scalpel.
5. Store in walk-in refrigerator while you prepare the sauce.

SIMPLE RED SAUCE

1. Blanch tomatoes in boiling Pellegrino water for 61 seconds.
2. Remove skins and seeds (if you don't have a wine press for this procedure but your feet are reasonably clean, stomp tomatoes in a 20-gallon Marthaware Bouillabaisser).
3. Strain through 300-denier-count silk taffeta.
4. Add spices.
5. Bring to a rolling boil, cook down to one pint.
6. Spoon a puddle onto each plate. If you run short, stretch with ketchup.
7. Carefully add calamari tips in a haphazard fashion, so they look like they just fell onto the plate.

Tender calamari tips, parboiled
and sautéed, rise up from a pool
of seasoned tomato sauce.

valentine's day

a romantic dinner for two

potage du vie

chilled oysters with powdered
rhinoceros horn

trussed rump roast

special dessert liqueur

Martha's patented pick-me-up

GLISTENING IN THE SOFT LIGHT of a
candle's glow, the magnificent swelling curve
of a massive rump roast strains mightily
against its golden bondage.

$\mathcal{P}$OTAGE DU VIE (SOUP OF LIFE)

The basic formula for this primordial soup dates back to antiquity and is reputed to have been used by Aphrodite. The recipe is derived from a Hedonite cookbook I found at a tag sale in Syria.

TO SERVE TWO

> 20 plump, overripe Italian tomatoes
> nonvirgin olive or flavored massage oil
> cayenne pepper or Spanish fly
> juice from one bushel of raw oysters
> one eyedropper full of she-goat heavy cream

1. After oiling your hands, squeeze tomatoes until they relinquish their seed.

2. Heat oil until it begins to smoke, then add tomatoes.

3. Sprinkle cayenne pepper and/or Spanish fly according to experience.

4. Let soup cool to body temperature.

5. Ever so slowly, add essence of oysters.

6. Deploy single drops of heavy cream on surface of the soup with eyedropper.

7. Using the tip of a Victorian hatpin, pull through each drop of heavy cream to form the tails of spermatozoan swimming unceasingly toward their goal.

8. Have several more drinks.

9. Serve soup to the object of your desire.

The straining majesty of a properly trussed rump roast is a wonder to behold and, when served steaming in a romantic setting, becomes the perfect metaphor for the timeless drama of chase and capture. A great piece of rump, strong materials and sufficient force are the keys to this experience.

First, beat the raw meat with a closed fist for 20 minutes every hour of the day before it is to be served. I have found that this works better than any chemical tenderizer on the market; after a day of abuse, the meat will take on a deep reddish hue that tells you it's fit to be tied. This method also has the added benefit of giving my deltoids and triceps a good workout.

Choosing the proper bondage material is also critical. I have always been partial to steel, brass or gold-plated titanium over common butchers' string, and for several reasons. First, when I bring my full force to bear, there isn't a piece of string in the world that will hold up. Furthermore, when a rump is bound in gleaming brass or gold it can be brought straight to the table and allowed to explode out of its chains directly in front of your guest. The exquisite tension and release of this presentation creates a memorable impression, however subconsciously, on most men. Lastly, I've found that the chain will stay hot for quite a while and can be put to good use after dinner.

t RUSSED RUMP ROAST

For best results, use the rump of a cow that has been overfed and never allowed to sit, thus leaving its muscles in a totally atrophied state. Meat this tender can be taken up in bare hands and eaten practically raw.

TO SERVE AND BE SERVED

> 1 four-pound rump roast from a freshly culled cow with measured fat content of 82 percent or more
> 1 pound eland butter
> high-tension, gold-plated chain

1. Using a stiff index finger, poke a hole into the center of the rump roast and work until it's the width of your wrist.
2. Insert the entire pound of butter (or as much as will fit) into the orifice.
3. Truss extremely tightly with chain, then lock *(see sidebar).*
4. Bake in a 2000-degree oven for six minutes, searing the outside while keeping the interior just warm enough to melt the butter.
5. Unlock and serve.
6. Pull apart and eat with bare hands (it is important to keep eye contact with your partner throughout this portion of the meal).
7. Shower (optional).

SPECIAL DESSERT LIQUEUR

This provocative cocktail was purportedly served by Casanova himself and has never failed me in my hour of need.

> 1 ounce Absinthe (a warning here: too much of this rare liqueur caused Vincent van Gogh to cut off his ear, so measure carefully)
> 1 ounce mineral oil
> juice of three bluepoint oysters
> 6 ounces home-distilled grain alcohol, 350-proof
> orange flower water to taste

1. Put all ingredients in a blender with shaved ice.
2. Pour mixture into shot glasses.
3. Serve in a ratio of three shots for him to one sip for you.

MARTHA'S PATENTED PICK-ME-UP

In the instance that your guest for the evening has exceeded his and/or your limit, this concoction is guaranteed to revivify him enough either to continue with the evening or drive home safely.

TO SOBER UP ANY HUMAN

> 1 ounce African Purple Zimbabwe coffee beans
> 1 ounce Madagascar desert-blooming foxglove
> 1 ounce Tabasco sauce
> liquid smelling salts
> Sweet'n Low to taste

1. Triple-brew the coffee until it reaches a caffeine content of 106 percent. Add foxglove, Tabasco sauce and Sweet'n Low. Pour into a Limoges demitasse cup.
2. Hold smelling salts under his nose. When he gasps, pour contents of cup down his throat. Stand clear.

CHILLED OYSTERS WITH POWDERED RHINOCEROS HORN

Used with great success by Cleopatra, Helen of Troy and Helen Gurley Brown, this age-old combination makes for a stimulating hors d'oeuvre and, hopefully, a satisfying evening.

TO SERVE ONE MAN

> 1 bushel of Madagascar red tip oysters from which the finest 12 have been selected
> politically correct, ranch-grown rhinoceros horn
> cayenne pepper or Spanish fly

1. Brush the outside of the oysters vigorously with a Portuguese brass wire brush to remove any Ebola virus present.
2. Touch up the shells of the oysters with a #10 sable watercolor brush using a wash of Ivory Black and Hooker's Green acrylic paint to achieve a uniform look.
3. Chill overnight to a temperature of 42 to 43 degrees.
4. Just before serving, put on your steel mesh glove and open the oysters using a tungsten-carbide bladed oyster knife. (See my catalog, product # 66345a-99742).
5. Serve open on a bed of shaved ice made from home-made water.

TOPPING

1. Take a one-ounce chunk of rhino horn and run it through a Bindorff high-speed blender until it's the consistency of "daytime cover-up" makeup or talcum powder.
2. Mix in equal parts of either cayenne pepper or Spanish fly, depending on how long you want the evening to last.
3. Lift each oyster gently and deposit 1/64-ounce of the mixture under the meat where he won't see it.
4. Watch closely while he eats the oysters. If he looks as if he's starting to get too "rambunctious," cut him off—or you'll never make it to the next course.

• romantic advice

MANY MIDDLE-AGED WOMEN report having trouble finding available men, but they've obviously never sought my advice:

1. Begin by looking in the right places. I frequent spots known for high numbers of susceptible males: beginner assertiveness training classes, 12-step co-dependency workshops, small men's stores, rubber clothing outlets.

2. Once you've selected a target, find out his favorite dishes. I have my staff locate his parents' home, then pay a visit late at night and go through his mother's recipe index card file. (This is also an excellent way to acquire new food ideas.)

3. Aphrodisiacs help establish an intimate mood, but I find them less reliable than alcohol. My rule of thumb is one drink every four minutes, a pace that usually leads even the most stalwart of men either to ardor or stupor.

4. Should both aphrodisiacs and alcohol fail, and your date heads for the door and freedom, use rope. A stout mooring line should give you the level of control you're after.

In the end, though, remember that there is no substitute for spontaneity. Just follow your instincts, or mine.

mother's day

homestyle dinner

& payback

tuna casserole with
potato chip topping

green bean & mushroom soup
casserole with onion rings

salisbury steak croquettes

sweet potatoes with
marshmallows

Jell-O aquarium mold

MOTHER-DAUGHTER RIVALRY reached its
peak in our family in the spring, when
Mother and I would compete in a friendly
bake-off to be judged by Father. Here I am
at 10 with my winning entry.

5

{Honoring Mother

As a rule, I treat Mother's Day like any other day of the year. In other words, there are 86,400 seconds in which to get everything done. If Mother happens to show up at one of my houses, and I happen to be in town and I don't have a lot on my plate that day, I try to squeeze her in for an appointment. This usually ends up in the form of some kind of playful cooking contest. She will attempt to make up a recipe and I will "try" to top it. Since I could out-cook Mother when I was six, and all the Cordon Bleu chefs in the world by the age of eleven, this is literally child's play for me. If no one on my staff or the media is watching, I sometimes even let her win. However, I have learned the hard way about losing at anything, even if it's on purpose and it's Mother's Day. In 1988, for instance, I "accidently" burned the top of an Apple Brown Betty to let Mother win that day's cook-off, which she then promptly leaked to the food critic at The New York Times, *who had a field day with it. It took me years to recover from that little generosity. I hope he's happy wherever he works now.*

SALISBURY STEAK CROQUETTES

Mother could stretch a little meat of questionable pedigree into an intriguing meal any day of the week.

TO KEEP FAMILY ALIVE

    1 pound dog, cat or other pet meat

    3 pounds used bread crumbs

    1 pound salt

    1 pound lard

    1 bunch parsley

    1 pail potatoes or other tubers

1. In a bucket combine all ingredients at once, then set on floor.
2. Using the business end of a 32-ounce Louisville Slugger, pound until the mixture coheres. (To check, toss in front of the dog. If he growls, cowers, whimpers, tucks his ears or tails, or runs off, it's ready).
3. Shape into croquettes with short, swift, vicious hits of the bat.
4. Melt lard in cast-iron skillet until it pops a foot or more above the stove.
5. Toss in croquettes and fry until safe to eat (about six hours).
6. Cover with a good ketchup.
7. Serve with a stack of airy white bread and quart bottle of any dark soda.

GREEN BEAN & MUSHROOM SOUP CASSEROLE WITH ONION RINGS

This classic '50s dish was served to me every Monday, Wednesday and Friday until I managed to leave home. It made a lasting impression but appears to have done little physical damage.

TO FORCE-FEED SIX CHILDREN

    1 package generic frozen green beans

    1 can condensed mushroom soup

    1 container dried onion rings

    homemade water

    2 tubs margarine

1. In a five-quart stew pot, boil frozen green beans for two hours or until mushy.

2. Strain beans in a colander, then let dry until they start to curl at the tips.

3. Add two quarts of water to one can of condensed mushroom soup. Cook down at a full boil until it's back to about a can's worth of soup.

4. Melt margarine in a saucepan and add onion rings. Allow them to sit for one hour until they absorb all the margarine and become a glutinous mass.

5. Dump all ingredients in a covered casserole dish, add the salt and bake with lid on for three hours at 350 degrees.

6. Uncover and place under broiler for 20 minutes to burn the top.

7. Transfer while hot to good Tupperware service.

8. Stand over children until all gone.

Jell-O played an important role in our home in Nutley when I was growing up. I remember Jell-O at every meal, and on special occasions all-Jell-O dinners; Christmases of Jell-O mold creches and ornaments for the tree; Jell-O baths, Jell-O dolls, Jell-O bicycles and once, when I was eight, a party dress made from lemon and lime aspic.

Recent studies have cited excessive early gelatin intakes as a leading cause of aggressiveness and self-aggrandizement in adults. But not so in our family. On the contrary, that early Jell-O discipline helped mold my siblings and me into the adults we are today: independent, ambitious and hungry for a world outside our Jell-O reality.

I think it only fair, then, to serve this timeless dessert to Mother whenever she visits.

Even on her day, Mother still tries to contribute in the kitchen.

*j*ELL-O AQUARIUM MOLD

Mother was endlessly fascinated by how many different ways she could serve us Jell-O, but this fish-in-aquarium version was probably her favorite.

TO SERVE AND SERVE AGAIN

a small cow

2 pounds white sugar

1 package yellow #27 food coloring

2 bags goldfish crackers

1 bag red fish gummies

1. Render the cow's bones in a 55-gallon oil drum, preferably somewhere downwind of the house.

2. After a day or so, skim off the gelatin.

3. Strain gelatin through 60 layers of linen cheesecloth to remove any microscopic bits of bone or gristle.

4. Boil purified gelatin in same oil drum.

5. Add sugar, food coloring and pour into mold. Refrigerate.

6. Check consistency constantly. When a tail feather from a blue mallard stands up firmly when blown on, it's time to add the goldfish.

7. Insert goldfish with surgeon's tweezers, orienting them so they swim in a natural manner.

8. Re-refrigerate overnight.

9. Place mold on a serving platter and blast gently with a acetylene blowtorch until it slips out of the mold.

10. Decorate with gummies and serve.

Goldfish-shaped crackers catch the late
afternoon sun as they "swim" endlessly
around the Jell-O aquarium made from
one of my extensive collection of
neo-Jersey, Depression-era molds.

4th of july

beach cookout

lobster au villain

freshly caught record striped bass
with cucumber scales

ragout of seaweed

Truman compote

LUMINARIES transform a lonely stretch of
beach at dusk into a dramatic cocktail and
barbecue staging area. They also prevent
anyone from even thinking about occupying
the same choice spot.

Poaching Lobster }

One of the reasons all of my homes are so close to the Atlantic Ocean is the bounty of fresh seafood that is there for the taking.

Of course, some of the best fish markets in the world can be found close by in New York; but for me, nothing matches the adrenaline rush of poaching.

Before first light, slip out of the house and make your way down to the beach, using Persian Gulf night-vision goggles to ensure that the beach is clear. Then untie the skiff and push off into the inky waters, softly motoring out to the first pots. Pull on the cold, wet line to haul the heavy, dripping wooden crate from the briny deep over the gunnels and behold what treasures Neptune has deposited during the night. It's like Christmas in July!

Poaching is not for the fainthearted, however. Readers would be well advised to follow some basic rules of thumb:

1. *Use a reliable boat equipped with a silent electric trolling motor and standby twin 75 h.p. Evinrudes for emergency getaways.*

2. *Wear sunglasses and wig or Sou'wester cap to avoid recognition and a hefty fine or jail term.*

3. *Make sure the boat is also equipped with a flare gun, which can be very effective at close range.*

4. *Always leave something in exchange in the lobster pot: collected seaglass bundled in a linen handkerchief; suntan lotion repoured into an attractive antique glass bottle and stoppered with a cork; a small jar of homemade tartar sauce.*

5. *Later in the day, as your guests speculate on the size and cost of dinner, you can finally relax as the evidence quickly disappears.*

*L*OBSTER AU VILLAIN

Cooked in a caldron of seawater over driftwood coals on the beach, poached lobster is far tastier than purchased or legally taken crustacea.

TO SERVE TWO DOZEN UNWITTING ACCOMPLICES

>   lobster pot of morning's catch
>   1 gallon drawn seacow butter
>   box of cherry bombs, ashcans, M80s and assorted
>   fireworks

1. Borrow pot of lobsters.
2. Change out of disguise and back into apron.
3. Store lobster in someone else's refrigerator until dinner.
4. Transport to beach in car with borrowed plates.
5. Cook in pit in sand covered with seaweed to avoid air surveillance.
6. Blow up pit with M80s and rake over lobster shrapnel before leaving beach.

*R*AGOUT OF SEAWEED

A combing of almost any beach will yield a cornucopia of legumes from the deep that are nutritious, delicious and priced just right for the cost-conscious hostess.

TO SERVE THE ENTIRE BEACH

>   kelp, polyps, sea cucumbers, etc.
>   bucket of brine
>   sea salt and spices

1. Hose down with seawater to loosen syringes, condoms, crack vials and other beach detritus.
2. Simmer in brine for 24 hours to detoxify.
3. Salt and spice to taste.
4. Serve on washed-up objects (shells, pieces of styrofoam and plywood, life vests, etc.).

*T*RUMAN COMPOTE (SEASONAL EAST HAMPTON FRUITS IN THEIR JUICES)

Fruits are always welcome at summer parties. Their sensual, casual tastes and witty, gustatorial repartee lighten any cocktail party or cookout. And, when glazed with alcohol, they do much to help lull guests after a long day on the beach.

TO SERVE SEVERAL DOZEN

1. Cruise local markets for young, fresh fruits that are firm but yielding to the squeeze.
2. Wash thoroughly before tasting.
3. Lubricate with juice and sweet liqueurs.
4. Peel, seed, slice and let sit in bowl of natural juices and alcohol for several hours.
5. Serve in glass bowls with napkins made from Calvin Klein underpants.

f

FRESHLY CAUGHT RECORD STRIPED BASS WITH CUCUMBER SCALES

After being stunned, caught, weighed, measured, photographed and officially recorded and documented, this world-record striper fed most of the people on the beach.

TO SERVE A LOT OF PEOPLE

    carbonium fly rod outfitted with 750-pound-test
       line and #90 stainless double-barbed Marlin
       hook on titanium leader
    2 gardeners in rowboats loaded with water mines
       and depth charges
    helicopter
    exceptional skill, determination, stamina and a
       1500-pound winch

1. Arrive at the beach before sunrise but just after the turn of the tide and eight cups of espresso.

2. Order gardeners to row out a mile and begin laying mines and dropping charges to guide fish toward you.

3. Have helicopter crew signal exact location of largest fish.

4. On 750-pound-test there won't be much of a fight, but if the fish is too big, tie the line to the winch, then to the tailhook on your Land Rover, and drag home.

5. Summon officials from the World Record Fishing Association and Guinness Book of Records.

6. Alert local and national media.

7. Scale, skin, gut, bone and dismember fish, then reassemble as if nothing had happened.

8. Steam in a French copper striped bass steamer for 31 minutes, then cool to beach temperature.

9. Slice 37 fresh cucumbers to 1/64th inch thickness.

10. Beginning from the tail, layer slices with a 1/4-inch overlap to replicate scales.

11. Rouse guests when ready and see to it that they eat.

all souls' day

a death at dinner
& *impromptu wake*

mortadeli on caskets
of toast

blackened Dead Sea
scallops

cold funeral meats

stiffened lady fingers
in ice cream

LIKE DEATH AND TAXES,
entertaining cannot be avoided. Even
the saddest of occasions calls for food that
is delicious, festive and beautifully
presented, such as these enchanting little
casket sandwiches.

{When a Guest Succumbs

Dying is one of the rudest things a guest can do during a dinner party. It completely disrupts the careful and rigid planning that must go into an occasion and is terribly unfair to the hostess.

However, should a guest give in to the temptation to leave the party early, a skillful hostess will always see to it that the remaining guests continue to enjoy one another's company .

I use the following checklist to cope with an entertaining challenge of this nature:

1. *Screen dinner guests for histories of heart ailments or serious diseases. Where possible, obtain copies of recent physicals or health insurance claim records.*

2. *When a guest hits the plate, keep conversation breezy and upbeat, referring to the corpse only when vital to an amusing anecdote or piece of gossip.*

3. *Immediately excuse the living, skip dessert, clear the plates and begin preparations for the wake. Make sure that none of the guests leaves the premises. Keep them occupied while you are preparing the body (weeding, harvesting, barn painting or some sort of aerobic exercise to restore their appetite is recommended). While this may seem harsh, entertaining etiquette dictates that the hostess facilitate this basic human rite.*

4. *Dead people can be used as attractive centerpieces, but not people who are too dead. Quickly, while you still can, shape and level the deceased's hand to hold a serving tray and begin setting out hors d'oeuvres. Next, arrange buffet platters around the body and stack plates on her midsection, which should be able to support them by this stage. Finally, as a thoughtful touch, place a bouquet of fresh flowers between her legs.*

Remember that no matter how much inconvenience a former guest has caused, a good hostess will always see to it that he or she be given a gracious farewell. It is equally important that family and friends remember the wake as another example of the hostess's unfailing performance in the face of adversity.

Homemade embalmsamic vinaigrette is siphoned directly into the deceased, who would have appreciated its zesty bite and tasteful packaging.

$\mathcal{M}$ORTADELI ON CASKETS OF TOAST

Mortadeli, or death loaf, is a provincial Sicilian meatlike food served to honor, or evoke, The Grim Reaper. Its rough texture, punctuated by random speed bumps of solid white fat, causes us to slow down and reflect on the fleeting nature of life.

TO SERVE A DOZEN BEREAVED

    1 entire pig
    1 mature belladonna plant
    assorted spices

1. Run a whole, boiled pig through a balogna grinder, extruding a fat, lumpy core of steaming pink meat.
2. Shred belladonna leaves and empty contents of spice rack onto butcher block. Roll meat in the stuff.
3. With a seed-planter, poke holes into the meat, then drop in globules of fat. Cover by tamping down with a hoe or the heel of a gardening clog.
4. Fist-stuff mixture into a length of donkey entrails casing, tying off ends with a double boatswain's knot.
5. When ready to serve, slap up on a high-speed slicer set at 1/16th of an inch.
6. Toast a loaf of white bread until nearly black, then cut into casket-shaped slices. Fill with sliced mortadeli.
7. Garnish with fresh belladonna.
8. Serve on a slab of mausoleum-quality marble.

Rigor mortis is just one of the challenges a hostess faces when organizing a wake on short notice. Here, the dead lends a hand in setting the table for a cold buffet.

*b*LACKENED DEAD SEA SCALLOPS

A traditional burial dish of the Essenes and other early peoples inhabiting ancient Israel, these delicious, slightly salty little mollusks make both a profound statement and a light repast.

TO SERVE WHOEVER STILL FEELS LIKE EATING

    4 dozen live scallops harvested from the Dead Sea

        or, if unavailable, from the Potomac

    6 dozen ground black peppercorns

    4 sticks clarified manatee butter

    1 quart can baby Arctic seal oil

    ripened fruit of a hot paprika bush

    2 jars onion & garlic powders

    36-inch diameter cast-iron scallop pan

1. Heat pan over high flame for two hours.

2. From the far side of the kitchen, toss in butter sticks and quart of oil.

3. Once flames have diminished to a safe height, add paprika berries and onion & garlic powders.

4. When the second flashover subsides, add scallops.

5. Cook for six seconds or until scallops stop moving, whichever comes first.

6. Toss contents and pan itself into backyard.

7. Serve wearing asbestos gloves.

{Building & Decorating a Coffin

Many years ago, when I was first starting out as a caterer and home entertaining consultant, I harvested a stand of virgin white pines on my Connecticut property, then laid the lumber up in my woodworking shop in the event that I might one day be called on to plan a funeral or cater a wake.

Happily (though sadly, too, of course), an opportunity to use the wood finally presented itself last fall. Should you find yourself facing a similar challenge, you'll want to keep the following in mind:

1. The older the wood, the more subtle and pleasing the results. But if you must use young, unseasoned lumber, first distress by shipping it to the Caribbean and exposing it to a few powerful storms or hurricanes. The beautiful patina on this wood was the work of Hugo.

2. Nails are cold, as well as unattractive. Instead, use traditional dovetail box joints at the corners, hardwood dowels, home-rendered glue and a brass piano hinge for the casket top.

3. Apply 10 to 20 layers of beeswax to the exterior surface (wait until bees in your apiary leave their hives shortly after sunrise, then borrow wax. They'll get over it.)

4. Upholster interior with a quiet chintz. I bartered a tray of my stuffed mushrooms for 50 yards of this fabric that was made for Louis XIV's "game wing" at Versailles.

5. Stencil, paint, carve or burnish an appropriate pattern on the outside of the coffin. In life, this particular person was quite talkative, so I used the Amish "Chatting Chicks" stencil pattern in her honor.

6. Following private interment, sneak the coffin back into the house for use as a blanket chest, winter bulb storage bin or conversational coffee table, as I do.

A simple stencil design on a hand-crafted coffin makes all the difference between an ex-guest resting in taste versus simply in peace.

christmas

holiday buffet

& ornament-making party

traditional Polish Christmas
wreath hors d'oeuvres

branded & roasted
limited-range wild turkey

snow peas, winter squash,
cold Brussels sprouts

Martha's eggnog

baba au rhum das

8

A PERFECTLY DECORATED
outdoor tree enhances property values
and induces holiday angst in visitors and
neighbors alike.

{Trimming the Trees

We hear so much today about the overcommercial-ization of Christmas, but a far graver concern is the general decline in America of decorating values and zeal. It wasn't always this way.

Growing up in New Jersey in the 1940s and '50s, I could barely wait for Christmas and the chance to outdecorate the other houses on our street.

Under my direction, my parents and siblings would erect a giant red plastic Santa with sleigh and reindeer on the roof, and a lifesize creche in the front yard, all bordered with blinking red and green lights. Then I'd climb the highest tree on the property and place a star made out of aluminum foil on the very top. My childhood dream was one day to decorate the White House tree.

While my tastes in ornaments have changed since then—I favor tiny white lights and a simple duet of red and gold ribbons, using Weyerhauser #30 ripstop wrapping ribbon capable of withstanding the elements and strong enough to use to rappel back down the tree—my values haven't. For me, the true meaning of Christmas remains competition and absolute victory.

The key to winning outdoor ornamentation is to view the property as an extension of the indoors. Given ample acreage, a backup power generator and underground cable with outlets at the base of each tree, one can decorate hundreds of trees and literally overwhelm the neighborhood.

But the real secret to my success outdoors is the lifelike ornamentation I use. Climbing out onto the uppermost branches of the highest evergreens, I spray-paint individual pine cones hanging from the tips without having to harvest and paint hun-dreds of them to hang indoors. And rather than labor to make silk and wire birds in nests of woven alfalfa (as I suggest that others do), I find it far more efficient to chloroform live birds, then gild them and their nests right in the trees.

*t*RADITIONAL POLISH CHRISTMAS WREATH HORS D'OEUVRES

In the old country, my relatives hung edible wreaths on their front doors for the villagers who remembered their address and came caroling on Christmas Eve. However, since people in Poland never answer the front door, only the rear, the wreaths were never consumed; instead, they froze until spring when they would thaw, rot and stink until finally discovered sometime in May and eventually burned, buried or picked clean by wolves. Today, I keep the spirit of this heart-warming tradition alive with seafood wreaths hung at my East Hampton homes.

TO SERVE THE NEIGHBORHOOD

3 feet coiled barbed wire	2 heads iceberg lettuce
needle-nose pliers	6 pounds shrimp
blowtorch	4 pounds Arctic scallops
solder and soldering iron	4 pounds Antarctic mussels
gluegun	2 jars Martha's Hot Sauce
2 heads winter kale	

1. Heat barbed wire with blowtorch and use pliers to bend into a 12-inch-diameter frame.
2. Bind kale and lettuce to frame with solder and soldering iron.
3. Impale seafood on barbs.
4. Glue crackers and pools of cocktail sauce to kale and lettuce.
5. Wire frame to doorbell so you'll know when visitors are nibbling (a mild shock will limit hors d'oeuvres to one per caller).

MARTHA'S EGGNOG

The holidays bring many people to my door, but none in such numbers as United Parcel Service drivers, who pick up and deliver late into the night.

In gratitude, I serve them this spirited drink and frequently wind up driving them home the next morning.

TO SERVE THE MEN IN BROWN

 1 gallon cognac

 1 gallon brandy

 1 gallon vodka

 1 quart crème de cacao

 1 quart crème de menthe

 1 quart triple sec

 4 dozen fresh brown eggs, separated

 2 gallons fresh heavy cream

 freshly harvested & grated nutmeg

 freshly harvested & grated cinnamon

 freshly caught & powdered Spanish fly

1. Upend all bottles at same time into bathtub when you see any deliveryman coming up the walk.

2. Toss in other ingredients.

3. Stir with foot.

4. Sprinkle surface of tub with nutmeg, cinnamon and Spanish fly.

5. Ask driver to deliver packages to bathroom.

BABA AU RHUM DAS

New Age friends love this updated, all-natural version of a traditional holiday cake.

TO YIELD TWO CAKES

 1 package active yeast infection

 1 cup warm gnu milk

 23/32nds cup field-harvested cane sugar

 10 large white ibis eggs

 1 pound sack hand-milled bulgur wheat flour

 1 teaspoon Indian Ocean salt

 6 sticks sacred cow butter

 fresh Himalayan sherpaberries for garnish

1. Butter a large crystal bowl, lick clean, rebutter.

2. Combine all ingredients and beat by hand until pliant.

3. Work dough by punching, kicking, elbowing and pummeling.

4. Cover with a damp washcloth and let sit overnight, occasionally visiting for short bursts of abuse.

5. Transfer to baking tins, then to a Baba au Rhum oven preheated to 350 degrees.

6. Bake while doing Hatha Yoga.

7. Serve hot to guests in the lotus position.

Brand Recognition }

With so may readers copying my preference for raising my own fowl, I've found it necessary to personalize my flocks by branding them shortly after they hatch. Branding birds, as well as other livestock and pets, is efficient, inexpensive and fun to do.

Naturally you can't use my brand, which is trade-marked and protected under penalty of really serious litigation, but you can follow my example.

This is how I brand things:
1. *Heat a #10 iron rod over an open fire until it turns a whitish red, then bend with welder's tongs to form your initials, logo, favorite symbol, etc.*
2. *Lure animals into forge barn or house with week-old brie and crudites platter.*
3. *Subdue with stun gun or tranquilizer darts.*
4. *Tie up, blindfold and gag.*
5. *Hold iron to left flank until brand is a golden brown. Brush with butter and repeat procedure on right.*

b RANDED & ROASTED LIMITED-RANGE WILD TURKEY

Nothing says Christmas in the country like a wild roasted fowl on the table. And with my trademarked brand on birds—turkeys, swans, Canada geese, pheasants, grouse, chickens, ducks, pigeons, blackbirds, mourning doves, mockingbirds, sparrows, chickadees, budgies, cockatoos, sapsuckers, parakeets or Emperor penguins—guests know that their dinner has been fed a perfect diet and lived a perfect life.

TO SERVE 80 CHILDREN & ADULTS
     herd of wild turkeys
     stuffing of stale bread, used newspaper,
        worn upholstery, etc.
     springbok butter
     parsley, sage, rosemary and thyme

1. Round up turkeys on motorcycle and herd into prep barn.
2. Kill them.
3. After plucking and gutting, stuff using high-compression air gun outfitted with "Stuffmaster" nozzle.
4. Lift skin and spell "Happy Holidays" in Baskerville typeface with basil leaves.
5. Rub with butter and herbs, being careful to leave personal brand exposed.
6. Preheat bird oven to 325 degrees and cook for a long time.

Teaching Children Holiday Crafts}

Christmas wouldn't be Christmas without a houseful of children. I love the sound of their little voices as they sing traditional field songs and make ornaments for the tree and gifts for my family, friends and business associates.

But young children by their very nature are lazy and undisciplined. They need, indeed crave, order and restraint. Children also need to reflect on the holidays and the role they are expected to play. Before they begin any project, therefore, I allow them some quiet time in a small containment shed at the edge of the property and, when I feel they're ready, escort them to the main house.

Once settled at the crafts table, it's merely a matter of keeping the children happy and motivated.

These are some suggestions:

- *Withhold affection and approval until all of the ornaments have been completed and checked by quality-control personnel.*

- *Serve low-sugar juices and delicious high-protein snacks, like soybean cookies or tuna packed in water, to enhance output. If it's still early and the children are sluggish, coffee or cappuccino may also be served.*

- *Never leave young children unsupervised. If an adult cannot be present, put something else in charge. Andy, my chow chow, loves children and is trained to maintain strict discipline in my absence.*

- *All kids will fidget, so it is permissible to use leg irons or other restraints.*

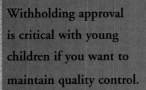

Withholding approval
is critical with young
children if you want to
maintain quality control.

REAL THANKS

To Lisa & Jack Connor, Linda Downey & Jacey Haskell, George & Del Grenadier, Richard & Betty Dorso, Tom & Gertrude Connor, Bill & Mary Jo Cornell, Kate Coleman, Mary & Anne Moffitt and Carol O'Rourke.

Special thanks to Susan Weinberg and Mauro DiPreta at HarperCollins.

Extra appreciation and very special thanks, as always, to the great Barry O'Rourke.

Thanks also to Laura Campbell of Campbell & Co. for page layout and art direction, and Joe Sequenzia; John Carafoli for food styling and terrific food, and Maggie Ellsworth of Classic Catering; Jack Rappoport, Esquire; and our Martha, the wonderful Suzy Pemberton.

Additional thanks to poolsiders Kelly Cornell, Sharon and Greg Rainey, Dean Builter, Stephanie Ingles and Martha Hibbs, and to David & Dylan Connor, Audrey Tumpowsky, Lynn Geane, Roger Huyssman, Ann Kavicky and Marsha Glazer; his "Holiness" Bill Pitt II, Bill Pitt III and Ginnie Cargill; gardener-fans Michelle Baldyga, Karren Bogle, Diane Fisk, Paula Jacobi, Sue Ryan, Bernelle Stephans, and to Jim Bleuer, Rob Wilbur and Mike "Mow" Kashetta; Valentine's Day dinner victim Joseph Sequenzia; mother & newborn Karen & Christopher Connelly; circumcision dad Peter Corrigan and David Messenger; Mother's Day mother and daughter Ann & Katrina Franzen; mourners Nancy Connor, John O'Hern, Judy and Jack Robson, Yvonne and Bill Huff, Stephanie Kirik, and to Lisa, Max & Decklin O'Hern and Liz Youngling; Donald Whittle, senior & junior, for master carpentry and model transportation; Compo Beach luminaries Rita Dennis, Corrine and Ted Youngling, Casey, Bill & Kimmy Coleman and Sunida Infahsaeng, and to Dick Alley and Southport Harbormaster Barbara Coburn; and Christmas child slave-laborers Jack Connor, Andrew Youngling, Billy & Steve Cargill, Megan Corrigan, Amy MacPherson, Kelsey Baker and Anne Wiswell.

Thanks, too, to John Savarino of Indulgence Patisserie; Terry Germaine of Germaine Tree Company; Rick Mola of Fisherman's World; Larry Protsko of Penthouse Wig Salon; John McStocker of John C. McStocker Antiques; Toby Welles of Design Core; Ester Johnston of The Johnston Modeling Agency; Glenn Oesterle and Nancy Mitchell of Village Hardware; John Faillace of Southport Center Barber Shop; Jack and Gerry Ringel of Switzer's Pharmacy; and Stanley Klein, merchant prince, of Klein's of Westport.

Finally, a sincere thanks to the nearly inimitable Martha Stewart, peerless stylist, entrepreneur and (to date) good sport, without whom this parody would not have been conceivable.